The Civil War

TURNING POINTS IN THE CIVIL WAR

Linda R. Wade

ABDO
Daughters & Publishing

Visit us at
www.abdopub.com

Published by Abdo Publishing Company, 4940 Viking Drive, Edina, MN 55435.
Copyright ©1998 by Abdo Consulting Group, Inc. International copyrights
reserved in all countries. No part of this book may be reproduced in any form
without written permission from the publisher.

Printed in the United States.

Graphic Design: John Hamilton
Contributing Editors: John Hamilton; Alan Gergen; Elizabeth Clouter-Gergen
Cover photos: John Hamilton; Digital Stock
Interior photos: Digital Stock
Illustrations: John Hamilton, pages 12, 17

Sources: *Atlanta.* Alexander, VA: Time Life Books, 1996; Barnes, Eric
Wollencott. *The War Between the States.* New York: McGraw-Hill Book Co.,
1959; *The Battle of Gettysburg.* New York: American Heritage, 1963;
Chancellorsville. Alexander, VA: Time Life Books, 1996; Davis, Burke.
Appomattox: Closing Struggle of the Civil War. New York: Harper & Row
Publishers, 1963; *Gettysburg.* Alexander, VA: Time Life Books, 1995; Jordan,
Robert P. *The Civil War.* Washington, D.C.: National Geographic Society, 1969;
Ray, Delia. *Behind the Blue and the Gray.* New York: Lodestar Books, 1991;
Reger, James P. *Life in the North During the Civil War.* Lucent Books: San
Diego, CA, 1991; Reger, James P. *Life in the South During the Civil War.* Lucent
Books: San Diego, CA, 1997; Sandler, Martin W. *Civil War.* New York:
HarperCollins Pub., 1996.

Library of Congress Cataloging–in–Publication Data

Wade, Linda R.
    Turning points in the Civil War / Linda Wade
        p. cm. — (The Civil War)
    Includes index.
    ISBN 1-56239-824-5
    1. United States—History—Civil War, 1861-1865—Campaigns—Juvenile
literature. I. Title. II. Series: Wade, Linda R. Civil War.
E470.W27 1998
973.7' 3—dc21   97-37476
                                                          CIP
                                                          AC

CONTENTS

INTRODUCTION

In the North, the raging battle for States' Rights was called the Civil War. The South, which called this terrible conflict "The War Between the States," wanted to preserve the institution of slavery. Leaders of the two sides thought the war would be a short and simple conflict, but it was now in its third year.

Thousands of men were killed in places like Manassas (Bull Run), Shiloh, Mechanicsville, Beaver Dam Creek, and Gaines Mill. Then came Antietam (an-tee-tem) on September 17, 1862. It was the bloodiest single day of the war. Twenty-two thousand men died. Thousands of horses and mules died. Farms and woods were made shambles. Still the war raged.

Poor communication caused generals to make wrong decisions. Attacks often came too late to end the war. Both the Union in the blue and Confederate in the gray were striving to build their armies for what they hoped would be one final push. The men were tired. They were homesick. They longed for loved-ones.

But there were to be two more years of war. Some of these battles were to be the most severe.

Facing page: D.W.C. Arnold, a private in the Union army.

CHAPTER 1

THE BATTLE OF CHANCELLORSVILLE

Before the Battle of Chancellorsville, Virginia, there was an important battle at Murfreesboro, Tennessee. It is often referred to as the Battle of Stones River. The Union army was marching south. Major General William S. Rosecrans was ordered to destroy the Confederate forces in Tennessee.

On the night before the battle, soldiers from both sides sat huddled in the cold darkness. Only a few yards separated them. The men began singing "Home Sweet Home" together to pass the time. It helped them forget the freezing temperatures.

The next day, December 31, 1862, the Confederates made the first move. Their attack went well. They charged through the thick cedar underbrush and sent the first two divisions of the Union right wing reeling backward.

Back and forth went the lines. One Union division ran out of ammunition and was forced to fall back. The Confederate forces burst through the gap in the line and the Northern forces fell back. The worst fighting occurred on the first day. However, it was not officially over until January 2. Confederate General Braxton Bragg finally retreated. Each side lost about one-third of its men. It became the battle with the highest casualty rate.

Back in Washington, D.C., President Lincoln was upset at General Ambrose Burnside and his disaster at Fredericksburg. He replaced Burnside with Major General Joseph Hooker. Hooker was known as "Fighting Joe." His first job was to raise the morale of the army. He did this by adopting a system of furloughs to stop desertions. Gradually, he rebuilt the spirit of the Union army until it was again ready to take to the field.

General Hooker arrived at Chancellorsville in the spring of 1863. He was more confident than ever of success. His Army of the Potomac numbered about 138,000 men. His operations so far had proceeded exactly according to plan. Most of the Union army was across the Rappahannock River. He had General John Sedgwick in place.

The mighty Confederate General Robert E. Lee was between them. Lee knew he was greatly outnumbered. He could have retreated. Instead, he devised a plan of surprise. Lee had General Stonewall Jackson attack the Union army. This attack confused General Hooker and he ordered a retreat.

An encampment of engineers from the Union's 8th New York State Militia.

Confederate dead behind the stone wall of Marye's Heights, Fredericksburg, Virginia.

That night Lee and Jackson talked. Their forces were outnumbered, but they had captured the initiative. They had to retain it. The decision reached that night was one of the great decisions of the war. The small Confederate army would divide into two parts. Jackson, with his three divisions, was to march around the right flank of the Union army and attack its right rear. Lee was to hold the present position with less than 20,000 men. He was to keep Hooker (who had four times as many men) occupied. Then he was to attack at the same time as Jackson.

It was quite a long march for Jackson's men. All day Lee waited. He wondered if Hooker would discover the movement and attack. But Hooker never did.

At 5:15 p.m., General Jackson looked at his watch. Then he calmly gave the order to advance. Loud and clear through the

Wilderness the Confederate bugles rang. The attack burst upon the Union army. Lee was also attacking on his front. Only darkness stopped the slaughter.

But that night tragedy struck the Confederacy. General Stonewall Jackson, while checking on his front lines, was shot by accident by his own men.

The same night that Jackson attacked the Union forces at Chancellorsville, Sedgwick received an order from Hooker to advance through Fredericksburg toward the rear of Lee's army at Chancellorsville. At daybreak his troops attacked Marye's Heights. At about noon, Sedgwick's men broke through and headed for Chancellorsville.

Later that afternoon, Sedgwick reached the Salem Church, one of the principal landmarks of the battlefield. Here he ran into a Confederate division of men sent by Lee.

That night more troops arrived, but Sedgwick escaped. General Lee then turned his army back toward Chancellorsville, but Hooker did not wait for him. He fled to safety across the river.

In the Battle of Chancellorsville, including the action at Marye's Heights and Salem Church, the Union losses (killed, wounded, captured, and missing) totaled about 17,000 men. The Confederate forces lost about 13,000 soldiers.

The greatest loss was General Stonewall Jackson. His left arm had to be amputated. Lee told Jackson's chaplain, "He has lost his left arm, but I have lost my right arm." Jackson started to get better, but then he caught pneumonia. He died on May 10.

General "Stonewall" Jackson.

CHAPTER 2

THE TRAGEDY OF GETTYSBURG

The Battle of Gettysburg began on June 3, 1863. General Lee and his 70,000 trained men started to move toward Pennsylvania. He divided his army into three parts. General Richard S. Ewell and his men led the way. Lee had decided to invade the North again. He still needed to gain foreign aid for the Confederacy. He also felt that a victory would convince the North that its efforts to subdue the South were useless. Northerners might then put pressure on their government to negotiate a settlement. He planned to capture a major Northern city.

In May 1863, Lee had obtained approval for his plan. The following month, he swung into action. His troops needed supplies that were only available in the North. In fact, one of the little skirmishes that started the Battle of Gettysburg actually began when some Southern soldiers tried to buy shoes there.

General Robert E. Lee, commander of the Confederate army.

Barlows' Knoll after the first day's battle at Gettysburg, Pennsylvania.

In the Northern ranks, President Lincoln knew he had to replace General Hooker. He selected Major General George G. Meade as the new commander of the Army of the Potomac.

There was no reason to believe that Gettysburg would be the scene of a major battle. It was just a quiet little town in Pennsylvania. However, several roads came together there. With so many military units moving north, it was possible that some sort of skirmish might occur. But when some small units clashed at Seminary Ridge on July 1, the major forces rushed in.

At first, the Union appeared to have the advantage. Not only were they more numerous than Lee's army, but they were on the high ground. Lee, however, had no intention of retreating.

On the second day Lee enjoyed a small measure of success. Sometime after 4:00 in the afternoon, a Confederate division came across the Devil's Den toward Little Round Top. It was a desperate struggle. Then the fighting went north into the Peach Orchard and the

Pickett's ill-fated charge on the third day at Gettysburg.

Wheatfield. They headed for Cemetery Ridge. Here they were met by a small Union regiment from Minnesota. A charge was ordered to plug a gap in the line. These brave Minnesota men fought against overwhelming numbers. In a matter of minutes, over 80 percent of them were dead or wounded. However, they had plugged the gap in the line. Even with this small Northern victory, the South had gained ground. Still, nothing decisive had been accomplished.

That night, Union General Meade called a council of his officers. They voted to fight it out at Gettysburg.

General Lee faced a difficult decision. The first two days had not gone badly, but supplies were running low. His men were tired, and the enemy was bringing up fresh soldiers. He had to choose between retreating to Virginia or making one final desperate effort to overrun the enemy lines. He decided on a final assault against the center of the Union lines. General George Pickett would lead the charge against Cemetery Ridge. The Union soldiers waited. Before the battle, Pickett wrote to his wife, "Oh, God in mercy help me as He never helped before."

The third day's battle began at daybreak. In some violent action, the Southern forces had to withdraw. There was a lull in the battle until afternoon. And then Pickett's men formed their line. He reminded them of their homes in Virginia. He reminded them of their wives, their children, and their mothers and fathers back home. Pickett told them to "fight for the state of Virginia!"

A harvest of death on the fields of Gettysburg. Over 50,000 men were killed or wounded during this decisive battle.

Off they marched across the open field. Fifteen thousand proud rebels advanced as if on parade. There was a half-mile of open, almost level, ground between the lines to cross; yet these men did not flinch. They knew the Yankees were waiting. They knew death would be the outcome for many. But they marched on.

Then it started—the yells, the gunfire, and the screams. Only a few of the men in "Pickett's Charge" went up the slopes of Cemetery Ridge. They were cut down. Barely half of the soldiers involved returned to Lee.

The Union had held.

General Lee withdrew to Virginia. Had General Meade pursued him, the war might have ended. He had 20,000 fresh reserves. Lincoln was angry that Meade had not followed Lee and put an end to the fighting and killing.

But the Battle of Gettysburg was over. It was probably the decisive battle of the war. In three days of fighting, 28,451 Southerners and 23,049 Northerners were killed or wounded. Never again was Lee able to assemble such a fighting force. His confidence was shattered. The Confederacy was at the lowest point in the war.

A sharpshooter's last sleep at the Battle of Gettysburg.

CHAPTER 3

THE SIEGE OF VICKSBURG

In the West, General Ulysses S. Grant spent the first months of 1862 and much of the first half of 1863 trying to capture the Confederate stronghold of Vicksburg on the Mississippi River. A line of hills follows the Yazoo River. Between these hills and the Mississippi is the Yazoo delta. Most of this land is very soft. To capture Vicksburg, the army would have to cross 175 miles of swamp.

Ulysses S. Grant.

It was wintertime. The weather was cold and rainy. Clothing, tents, bedding, and supplies stayed wet most of the time. Malaria and smallpox broke out among the troops.

General Grant made four attempts to capture Vicksburg by land. It was impossible. He decided upon a siege. Union ships and troops stopped food shipments to the city. It was so bad that the people even caught rats and cooked them.

Meanwhile the city was being shelled. The Confederates returned the fire. But by July 4, Vicksburg surrendered. The Union now had full control of the Mississippi River.

This was a real blow to the South. Confederate President Davis had considered Vicksburg his most important stronghold.

CHAPTER 4

THE BATTLE OF CHICKAMAUGA AND CHATTANOOGA

The Union had control of the Northeast and the West with the victories at Gettysburg and Vicksburg. But still the Confederacy fought on.

Now the war turned to the various cities and places in the South. One battle was at Chickamauga. It was located on Chickamauga Creek near the Tennessee-Georgia state line. Union General William S. Rosecrans and his Army of the Cumberland were on their way to Chattanooga. This town, nestled in the mountains, was important because it had several railroad interchanges. It also had the Tennessee River to carry supplies.

Confederate General Bragg learned of the advance. He remembered his defeat six months before at Stones River. He needed a victory. Shortly after dawn on September 19, he savagely attacked the Union army at Chickamauga.

The next day a gap opened in the Union ranks. The Confederates roared through. Only one Union line held. It was under the control of General George H. Thomas. He was given the nickname of "The Rock of Chickamauga."

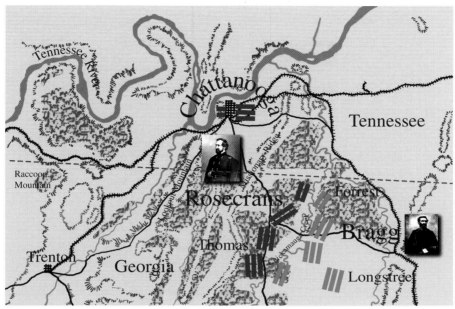

Day one of the Battle of Chickamauga.

It was soon apparent that the South was in control. In addition to having won the battle, the Confederates captured thousands of small arms and 51 guns. Bragg had his victory.

It would be the last important victory for the Confederacy. The cost in lives was high. Confederate losses totaled more than 18,000 out of 66,000 total men. Union losses were 16,000 out of 58,000. An Alabama unit lost 55 percent of its soldiers and almost half of its officers. Fighting in the woods had been very deadly.

The Union army retreated to Chattanooga. Instead of chasing them, General Bragg decided to lay a siege and force them to surrender. High mountains surrounded the city, so he had troops stationed in all the key positions. Lookout Mountain was one of them. Meanwhile the North was rushing reinforcements to General Rosecrans. General William Tecumseh Sherman left Mississippi. He had a large force from the Union Army of the Tennessee.

Almost a month after the Battle of Chickamauga, General Grant was placed in command of all the Union forces in the West. General Thomas replaced Rosecrans.

Then General Bragg made a big mistake. He divided his army and sent part of it to Knoxville, Tennessee. General Grant took advantage of this. He opened the "Cracker Line," a supply route.

There were three battles. The first battle was on November 23, 1863, at Orchard Knob. The second was on the following day at Lookout Mountain. In some places the side of the mountain was so steep that the attackers had to use scaling ladders to reach the top.

The Battle of Missionary Ridge was fought on November 25. The Union, with its six divisions, could not dislodge one Confederate division. The South was determined. In some places the ridge was so steep that their cannon could not shoot downhill. They rolled boulders and cannonballs down on the attackers. After hours of fierce hand-to-hand fighting, the Union troops withdrew.

The next day, General Thomas and his men started out by climbing the steep mountainside. The rebels could see them coming. There were thousands. The Confederates were outnumbered. The blue mass kept coming. The Army of the Tennessee panicked and ran. They had never run before, but the pressure of the moment was too much.

With this victory, the North had control of the city and nearly all of Tennessee.

Cutting a telegraph wire to disrupt the enemy's communications.

CHAPTER 5

THE VIRGINIA CAMPAIGN

What was it going to take to end this war? President Lincoln saw in Ulysses S. Grant the leader he had sought throughout the entire war. On March 9, 1864, Lincoln promoted Grant to lieutenant general, giving him command of all Northern armies.

Grant was determined to bring the war to an end. He would go with the Army of the Potomac and General George Meade to northern Virginia. They would try to capture Richmond. He knew he was up against the brilliant Robert E. Lee. General William T. Sherman would advance from Chattanooga into the Atlanta Campaign. His task was to destroy the South.

The main campaign was between Lee's Army of Northern Virginia and Meade's Army of the Potomac. Lee only had about 62,000 men, while Meade's men totaled 110,000. The campaign opened shortly after midnight on May 4. General Grant had his men marching at night. They were going through tangled undergrowth. He hoped to get through this dense forest before he met Lee. However, Lee guessed this move. He knew he could not beat the Union armies in the open field. So he settled into an area known as the Virginia Wilderness.

The underbrush was so thick that the soldiers could not see ahead. The result was two days of furious and confused fighting under terrible conditions. It was impossible to see and control troop movements. Men fought blindly. They could not see where their shots were going. In fact, Confederate General James Longstreet was shot by his own men. Then the smoldering hot shells started the woods on fire. Many wounded men died in the flames.

Always before the Army of the Potomac had retreated when it had been partially defeated. Not this time. It advanced instead. One battle led right into another. The gunfire never stopped.

On the night of May 7, General Grant moved toward Spotsylvania. However, Lee's army was already there. This battle became one of the most intense of the entire war. During the next 12 days several assaults were made upon the Confederate defenses. The Union losses mounted higher and higher. They were much greater than those of the Confederates, but the Union forces had replacements. Lee's army was steadily growing weaker. There were too few men left in the South to fill his ranks.

The North continued marching. There was a fierce battle at Yellow Tavern, north of Richmond. Confederate General Jeb Stuart was killed. Then another movement brought the forces together at Cold Harbor on June 3. This was a little community north of Richmond. Grant was determined to smash the Confederate army. To do this, he would have to cross open ground under heavy Southern

fire. The men knew it would be another terrible battle. The night before, they sewed their names and addresses in their coats, hoping that someone would let their families know where they died. The battle resulted in a loss of about 7,000 men in one hour. General Grant always regretted his decision to attack.

General "Jeb" Stuart.

The misery of trench warfare at Petersburg, Virginia.

In one month of fighting, Grant had lost almost 40,000 men. Newspapers were calling him "Butcher Grant." He knew he had to change his tactics. He decided to make one more try to finish the war. He was going to Petersburg, 23 miles south of Richmond. This was the supply hub of all the railroads for Richmond.

The men had to cross the James River. To do this, the Union army built a bridge consisting of 101 pontoons. Despite numerous attacks on Petersburg, they could not break through Confederate defenses. Grant finally decided on a siege. It began on June 20, 1864. They cut one railroad supply route leading south and one leading west. Northern soldiers stretched out and around the city. Then, on July 30, a regiment of Pennsylvania coal miners exploded a mine beneath a Confederate strongpoint. The blast made a crater 170 feet long, 60 feet wide, and 30 feet deep. Thousands of soldiers dropped into the crater. They were targets for a Confederate counter-attack.

The Union army continued to tighten its hold. Food became scarce. The women had no needles to sew clothes. It was a long and cold winter. The end did not come for over nine months. But finally, on April 2, the Army of Northern Virginia fled Petersburg.

No. 301. RAILROAD MORTAR AT PETERSBURG, VA.,
July 25, 1864.

A Union railroad mortar used at the siege of Petersburg.

CHAPTER 6

SHERMAN'S MARCH THROUGH GEORGIA

While General Grant and his soldiers were pressing through Virginia, General Sherman headed for Atlanta, Georgia.

On June 27, Sherman met General Joseph E. Johnston and his Army of the Tennessee at Kennesaw Mountain. Once again, soldiers had to deal with steep slopes, woods, and tangled undergrowth. When the Union formations came to an open field, they were met with bullets and cannonballs. "The enemy came within five feet of our breastworks and the slaughter was terrific as our troops literally mowed them down," remembered one Confederate. Hand-to-hand fighting took place. However, in the end, it was a Union victory.

During the time of these battles, Abraham Lincoln was running for his second term as president. Confederate leaders felt that if Lincoln was defeated in the November election, the war might be stopped.

Now General Sherman became aggressive. He was headed to Atlanta. Then he would make a sweep of the South. The leaders knew it would be difficult. Sherman needed to attack the Confederates almost daily. He would destroy the South's capacity to wage war. Then he would swing up through South Carolina and on into Virginia.

Confederate President Jefferson Davis was aware of his dwindling forces. Still, he pushed forward. General Johnston was

Confederate earthworks and fortifications ringing Atlanta.

relieved of his command. In his place was General John B. Hood. He was a brave man. He had lost an arm at Gettysburg and a leg at Chickamauga. He had to be tied to his horse each morning. He took advantage of situations and seemed to know when to move. On July 20, his men suffered heavy losses north of Atlanta at Peachtree Creek. The Union commanders did not expect another attack. In fact, General Sherman received information that led him to believe that Atlanta was being evacuated. He issued orders for a pursuit.

Instead of running, General Hood withdrew his troops into bunkers already prepared for the defense of Atlanta. These bunkers made it very difficult for Sherman to go anywhere. On the night of July 21, an attack was planned. Confederates came from behind with tremendous force. They were to be reinforced with a frontal attack. However, there was enough of a delay between the two attacks that the Union was able to overcome the Confederates. If Hood had moved both lines at the same time, the result would have been a resounding Union defeat.

Now the Union forces closed in around Atlanta. There was another Confederate attack. After this battle, Sherman waited to move. He bombarded the city for several days. He destroyed the railroads and cut off supplies.

It took until September 1 to defeat General Hood and his army. Before they left the city, the Confederates blew up their much-needed supplies. There was no way they could carry these supplies with them. As they left, billows of smoke and fire filled the night air.

General Sherman and his men entered Atlanta on September 2. The four-month long campaign had taken a harsh toll on Sherman's army. The men set up tent cities. Then they ordered every man, woman and child to leave the city. Before he left on November 15, Sherman ordered Atlanta to be set on fire. It was a sad day for the South.

Before Atlanta, President Lincoln's re-election seemed unlikely. This victory gave hope to the president.

General Sherman now moved south. Sixty-two thousand men in four columns began to march. The troops lived off of what they found. They did this by looting and destroying farms, crops, and plantations. They left a path of ruin and destruction. As the soldiers came to homes, all the people were ordered out. The homes were burned. Pigs and cows became meat for the army. Gardens were raided.

Rails from the railroads were heated and then twisted. What they could not use, they burned. They even looted the slave cabins. Cotton was burned. Fear crossed Georgia as the Union army marched 425 miles. Destruction was in every step.

Sherman emerged at Savannah in December. Then he turned his troops to go through South Carolina. They were even harder on the people of South Carolina. This had been the first state to secede. Charleston was destroyed. It was nothing but a ruined garden of weeds and widows. Meanwhile, hundreds of desperate Confederates were leaving the army. Richmond finally gave General Lee a battalion of black troops.

In Washington, D.C., Abraham Lincoln had won the election with 55 percent of the popular vote. Only Kentucky, Delaware, and New Jersey had not voted for him. He vowed to end slavery and bring the country back together.

The ruins of an Atlanta factory and ammunition train.

CHAPTER 7

THE END COMES AT LAST

Not only had armies fought against each other, but also both the Confederate and Union navies had fought many battles. While the *Monitor* and *Merrimac* had been the first ironclad ships, many more were added. These ships had secured harbors. They had bombarded cities. They had been a part of several sieges.

Both General Grant and General Lee knew the war must end. The siege at Petersburg had all but starved the Confederate army. Sickness, disease, and desertion cut deeply into Lee's ranks.

The last push came on March 25, 1865, at Fort Stedman, near Petersburg. Lee's army attacked the Union lines. The Southern troops captured Fort Stedman. However, Grant's reserves arrived and pushed Lee's men back.

General Grant quickly followed this success with huge attacks all along the Petersburg line. Lee's men could not stand up against such odds. Grant kept up the chase. On April 6, he attacked Lee's army at Sayler's Creek. The fighting that day cost Lee 7,000 causalities. That was one-fourth of his army.

Three days later, General Lee and his Army of Northern Virginia reached Appomattox Court House. They found themselves surrounded by Grant's Union troops. Lee realized that the war was lost. Continued fighting would mean useless loss of life. He told one of his generals that there was nothing to do but go to General Grant.

The McLean's House, Appomattox Court House, Virginia.

He wrote a note asking Grant for an interview. He was ready to talk about terms of surrender.

On April 9, 1865, General Lee and General Grant met in a house in the little settlement of Appomattox Court House, Virginia. It was Palm Sunday. Grant appeared in a mud-splattered private's coat. Three stars indicating his rank were plainly visible on the shoulder strap. Lee came in his best uniform with a dress sword on his side. The meeting lasted two hours.

Grant offered to send the soldiers home instead of to prison. He gave them their horses so they could plant their fields. Officers could keep their side arms. He also fed the hungry men. The two gentlemen shook hands and signed the agreement. The war was over. It was 3:00 p.m., almost four years to the day after the war had begun. General Grant announced, "These men are our countrymen again."

General Lee told his men, "Boys, I have done the best I could for you. Go home now. If you make as good citizens as you have soldiers you will do well. I shall always be proud of you. Good bye and god bless you all."

A few weeks later, the last of the Confederate army surrendered; the long years of war were over.

INTERNET SITES

Civil War Forum
AOL keyword: Civil War

This comprehensive site on America Online is a great place to start learning more about the Civil War. The forum is divided into four main groups. In the "Mason-Dixon Line Chat Room" you can interact with fellow Civil War buffs. The "Civil War Information Center" is especially good for historians and reenactors, and includes help with tracking down your Civil War ancestors. The "Civil War Archive" is full of downloadable text and graphic files, including old photos from the National Archives. When you're ready for more in-depth information, the "Civil War Internet" group provides many links to other sites.

The United States Civil War Center
http://www.cwc.lsu.edu/civlink.htm

This is a very extensive index of Civil War information available on the Internet, including archives and special collections, biographies, famous battlefields, books and films, maps, newspapers, and just about everything you would want to find on the Civil War. The site currently has over 1,800 web links.

These sites are subject to change. Go to your favorite search engine and type in "Civil War" for more sites.

PASS IT ON

Civil War buffs: educate readers around the country by passing on interesting information you've learned about the Civil War. Maybe your family visited a famous Civil War battle site, or you've taken part in a reenactment. Who's your favorite historical figure from the Civil War? We want to hear from you!

To get posted on the ABDO & Daughters website, E-mail us at "History@abdopub.com"

Visit the ABDO & Daughters website at www.abdopub.com

GLOSSARY

Amputate
Cut off.

Army of the Potomac
Primary army of the Union.

Bunker
Mound of dirt or a trench used for protection from gunfire.

Confederate Army
Southern army.

Confederate States of America
Eleven states that withdrew from the United States in 1860-1861. These states included Alabama, Arkansas, Florida, Georgia, Louisiana, Mississippi, North Carolina, South Carolina, Tennessee, Texas, and Virginia.

Desertion
Leave the army without permission.

Emancipation Proclamation
A proclamation by President Lincoln stating that from January 1, 1863, all slaves in the territory still at war with the Union would be free.

Furlough
A period of time when a soldier had permission to leave the fighting troops.

Rebels
Confederate soldiers.

Retreat
The act of going back, usually used in defeat.

Richmond

Richmond, Virginia, the official capital of the Confederate States.

Union

Another name for the United States. Twenty four states remained loyal to the Union during the Civil War.

Washington

Capital of the Union. Part of the District of Columbia, which at the time of the Civil War included the cities of Washington and Georgetown. In 1895, Georgetown was annexed (added, or absorbed), and Washington became more commonly known as Washington, D.C.

Yankees

Union soldiers.

Officers of the 69th New York Infantry at Fort Corcoran.

INDEX